D1505950

How To Convince Your Parents You Can...

Care For A Pet Racing Pigeon

Tammy Gagne

Mitchell Lane

PUBLISHERS

P.O. Box 196

Hockessin, Delaware 19707

Visit us on the web: www.mitchelllane.com

Comments? email us: mitchelllane@mitchelllane.com

Mitchell Lane

PUBLISHERS

Printing   1   2   3   4   5   6   7   8   9

A Robbie Reader/How to Convince Your Parents You Can...

Care for a Kitten	Care for a Pet Mouse
Care for a Pet Bunny	Care for a Pet Parrot
Care for a Pet Chameleon	**Care for a Pet Racing Pigeon**
Care for a Pet Chimpanzee	Care for a Pet Snake
Care for a Pet Chinchilla	Care for a Pet Sugar Glider
Care for a Pet Ferret	Care for a Pet Tarantula
Care for a Pet Guinea Pig	Care for a Pet Wolfdog
Care for a Pet Hamster	Care for a Potbellied Pig
Care for a Pet Hedgehog	Care for a Puppy
Care for a Pet Horse	Care for a Wild Chincoteague Pony

Library of Congress Cataloging-in-Publication Data
Gagne, Tammy.
    Care for a racing pigeon / by Tammy Gagne.
        p. cm. — (A Robbie reader. How to convince your parents you can—)
    Includes bibliographical references and index.
    ISBN 978-1-58415-801-1 (library bound)
    1. Racing pigeons—Juvenile literature. I. Title. II. Title: How to convince your parents you can— care for a racing pigeon.
    SF469.G33 2010
    636.5'96—dc22

                                                                            2009027355

ABOUT THE AUTHOR: Tammy Gagne is a freelance writer who specializes in the health and behavior of companion animals. She is the author of numerous books for both adults and children, including *How to Convince Your Parents You Can Care for a Pet Wolfdog* for Mitchell Lane Publishers. She lives in northern New England with her husband, son, dogs, and parrots.

TABLE OF CONTENTS

Words in **bold** type can be found in the glossary.

Racing pigeons are smart pets. To hold one, gently cup your hands around its body with its wings closed.

Chapter One

OFF TO A FLYING START

Imagine attending your first pigeon race. In your hands you hold your beloved bird. Soon you will release your pet into the wind, trusting that it will return. Will your pigeon win the race? Will it indeed find its way back home to you? Being part of the sport of racing pigeons can be thrilling, rewarding, and scary all at the same time.

Many people all over the world own pigeons. Some owners enter their birds in shows where judges pick the best-looking birds. Other owners train their pets for races with other pigeons that span hundreds of miles. These birds are commonly called racing pigeons.

Most people have seen **feral** (FAYR-ul) pigeons, which are a common sight in most cities. The idea of keeping one of these pigeons as a pet may seem a little strange, but racing pigeons are bred to be much

Hand-feeding helps keep pet racing pigeons tame.

tamer than these wild pigeons. Most wild pigeons will fly away if you walk toward them, but racing pigeons are used to being handled by humans.

One of the most exciting parts of owning a racing pigeon is the amount of freedom you can give your pet. Unlike most other pets, a racing pigeon does not have to be contained in a pen or attached to a leash to be kept safe. You can give this amazing animal its complete freedom by racing it.

You may have heard racing pigeons called homing pigeons. This is because these birds possess an instinct to return home from virtually anywhere.

They can fly as fast as 60 miles per hour and travel 500 miles or more in a single day.

In races, pigeons compete against each other to fly home as quickly as possible. No one knows for certain how these amazing birds locate their home when flying. It is almost as if each one has its own compass or GPS system built into its

fun FACTS

Pigeon racing is the national sport of Belgium.

aerodynamic body. Some scientists think that pigeons can somehow detect the earth's magnetic field and utilize it much like a compass does—always "feeling" which way is north. Others think they may watch the position of the sun to help find their way home.

Training a racing pigeon takes time and knowledge. Pigeon **fanciers** (FAN-see-erz) both young and old participate in the sport. Still, convincing your parents that you can care for a pet racing pigeon may be difficult. The best way to get your parents to say yes to your request is by learning as much as you can about these fascinating birds. By doing so, you can show your parents that you would make a responsible racing pigeon owner.

Sergeant Harry Lucas holds his homing pigeon G.I. Joe, who earned the Dickin Medal for **Gallantry** in World War II. G.I. Joe was the first American animal to receive this honor.

Chapter Two

LEARNING MORE ABOUT RACING PIGEONS

People began racing pigeons in the early 1800s. These birds have been used as message carriers for much longer, though. It is believed that pigeons carried messages in Persia and North Africa as many as 5,000 years ago. Later, pigeons were used in the empire of Genghis Khan in Asia and to announce the winners of the early Olympic Games in Greece.

Pigeons have also played a key role in many of the world's major wars. Roman emperor Julius Caesar used pigeons more than 2,000 years ago to send messages home from battle.

A pigeon named G.I. Joe saved the lives of a thousand British soldiers in World War II. This bird carried a message informing the British army that they were about to bomb their own troops. G.I. Joe arrived at his destination just a few minutes before this terrible disaster would have taken place.

Modern racing pigeons do not carry messages. Instead, birds get fitted with a new electronic band before each race. These bands contain a computer chip that identifies the pigeons. Each bird's chip also records when it crosses the finish line at the home coop. Some races are won by just seconds or milliseconds!

Races can span as little as 100 miles or as many as 1,000. Longer races can have hundreds of participants. The pigeons are released at the same time and fly to their individual homes. A bird's final score is measured in yards per minute. This makes the contest as fair as possible, since some birds need to travel farther than others. A fast pigeon may travel up to 1,700 yards per minute. (That's about 60 miles per hour!)

*fun*FACTS

In 2008, a racing pigeon named Boomerang returned to the man in England who raised her—10 years after he had given her away. She flew more than 1,200 miles to get there. Boomerang was 13 years old at the time of her incredible journey!

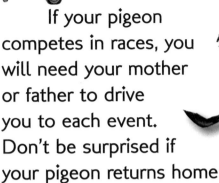

If your pigeon competes in races, you will need your mother or father to drive you to each event. Don't be surprised if your pigeon returns home before you do. Even if you start heading back immediately after the release, your bird will almost certainly be waiting to welcome you home by the time you get there.

Like all athletes, racing pigeons must be trained. An owner begins by allowing his or her bird to fly around outside the home. Then the owner ventures a bit farther from home, and then maybe about a mile away, before releasing the bird. As the bird gets better and quicker at finding its way home, the owner can move farther and farther away before releasing it. Some owners go as many as 50 miles or more away from home while training their pet racing pigeons.

Of course, this kind of workout requires a fit body. Although they may look stout, pigeons are surprisingly lean. Their long wings and short tails also make it easy for them to fly. Pigeons measure about 13 inches (33 centimeters) from bill to tail. They weigh about a pound (half a kilogram). Males are usually a bit larger than females.

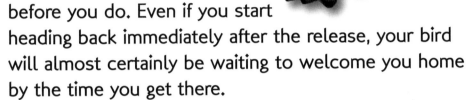

Racing pigeons usually lay two eggs, a couple of days apart.

Both males and females play a big role in rearing baby pigeons, which are called **squabs** (SKWOBZ). Males carry small twigs one at a time to the females, who make the nests. The female then lays two white eggs. The parents take turns keeping these eggs warm until they hatch about 18 days later. One of the unique things about pigeons is that both parents produce special milk they feed the squabs.

Squabs are born blind. After a few days, they can open their eyes. Squabs have brown or gray-brown eyes. Adult pigeons have orange eyes.

Wild pigeons have a lifespan of about five years. Many are killed by hawks and falcons, their biggest predators. When kept as pets, though, many pigeons can live fifteen years or more. If you are thinking about getting a racing pigeon as a pet, know that you could be in for a very long trip indeed.

Most birds drink water by sipping it and then throwing their heads back. This causes the water to slide down their throats. Pigeons, however, use their beaks to suck up water, much like straws!

FINDING A RACING PIGEON

Many racing pigeon owners breed their own birds, but anyone can purchase pigeons for racing. People throughout the United States offer racing pigeons for sale. Prices range significantly. You can pay anywhere from twenty-five to thousands of dollars for a single bird. Pigeons that have been trained well cost much more than others.

Most racing pigeon owners have at least several birds, but you can certainly own just one. In fact, caring for a single bird is a smart way to get started in this pastime. You can then add birds one or two at a time to make sure you don't become overwhelmed. You must never acquire more birds than you can realistically care for.

Your nearest racing pigeon club is a great place to visit when searching for your first racing pigeon. Club members can help answer any questions you may have about these birds. Some of them may even breed birds for sale. People involved in pigeon racing often say one of the best things about the hobby is the great friends they have made. Most are more than willing to help out someone new to the sport.

Pigeons come in 28 different color types called **morphs**. The most common morph is called a blue bar. These birds have two black or dark gray stripes (that look like bars) on each of their light gray wings. They have dark gray bodies and neck feathers that look a bit like rainbows in the light.

Certainly, you may prefer the look of one bird to another. But appearance should never be your first priority. What is most important is that you buy a healthy bird from a responsible breeder. Good breeders keep their pigeon **lofts** clean. They also feed their birds fresh, healthy foods and exercise the birds regularly.

The best time to get a racing pigeon is when it is young. A baby racing pigeon will **wean** at about 28 to 35 days of age. It will **fledge** (FLEDJ) by six weeks. At this time, it may be adopted. This will help ensure that the bird will fly back to you instead of to its breeder when it comes time for racing. More than one racing pigeon has been known to return to its previous owner when placed in a new home.

If you plan to enter your bird in races, look for a bird that shows good potential for flying ability. Most

Seven Common Pigeon Morphs

Blue Bar Pigeon

Red Bar Pigeon

Spread Pigeon

Red Pigeon

Pied Pigeon

White Pigeon

Checker Pigeon

breeders can spot these birds in their flocks, but there are no guarantees that any bird will ever win a race. Beware of any breeder who makes such promises.

Above all else, owning a racing pigeon should be fun. You will spend far more time working with your pet than you will spend racing it. For this reason, you should always choose a bird with a good personality. Always approach a bird slowly so that you don't frighten it. If a bird nips at you or seems extremely fearful, keep looking.

A pigeon loft should provide air, sunshine, and shade.
Always wash your hands after handling a racing pigeon.
Some diseases that strike pigeons can be passed to
humans.

CARING FOR A RACING PIGEON

One of the best things about pigeons is that they can survive in almost any climate. Just like wild pigeons, racing pigeons can live anywhere in the continental United States. They do, however, need proper shelter no matter where they reside.

In addition to a roof and four walls, a pigeon loft must provide each bird with daytime sunlight. Most pigeon lofts include a flight area where the birds can spend time in the sun. Like people, pigeons need sunshine to remain healthy, because sunshine provides vitamin D. For birds, this vitamin helps grow healthy bones and feathers. Vitamin D is also important for **reproduction** (ree-proh-DUK-shun).

Pet racing pigeons also need a safe place to sleep at night. If you live in an area where raccoons or weasels could pose a threat to your birds, you must make sure your loft is secure. No matter how fast your

Be sure to build many perching spots inside your pigeon loft. Don't make the ceiling too high. An overly high ceiling will make it difficult for you to catch your birds.

birds are, they are no match for these crafty natural predators inside a cage.

You can buy a loft or make one yourself. If you decide to make one, buying a kit will make the process a lot easier. Most lofts are about the size of a large garden shed. Place your loft on a well-lit area of your property. It should be close enough for you to hear if a predator tries to force its way inside it. If you live in a city, you may be able to place a small loft outside on a patio.

Your loft should protect your bird from extreme temperature changes and moisture. If you live in a humid climate, you may need to use a machine called

a **dehumidifier** (dee-hyoo-MIH-duh-fy-er) to remove excess moisture from the air. Good **ventilation** (ven-tih-LAY-shun) is also important. The air inside the loft should be as fresh as the air outside. You should clean the loft weekly with bleach and water to kill any germs that could make your pet sick.

To help keep your racing pigeon healthy, you must feed it nutritious foods. Most birds love to eat seeds, but an all-seed diet is full of fat and not very nourishing. Healthy foods include grains like wheat and barley. Even these are not enough, though. Other important foods rich in nutrients include oats and

If you own a lot of racing pigeons, you will need a trailer to take your birds to races. Racing clubs may also own trailers.

legumes like peas and lentil beans. Most vegetables are also great choices. Avoid feeding pigeons Brussels sprouts, cauliflower, broccoli, and cabbage, though. These foods can make your bird sick. A racing pigeon also needs a water bowl at least an inch deep.

*fun*FACTS

You should wash your bird's feet and feathers when it returns home from a race. This will help remove any germs your bird may have picked up during its trip.

The most successful racing pigeon owners agree that diet and exercise play the biggest parts in training winning birds. If you plan to

Pigeon is another word for rock dove. Couples often release white homing pigeons at their weddings. They believe it will bring peace, love, and faith to their marriage.

When cleaning a racing pigeon loft, it is very important to remove droppings from all surfaces. This helps to prevent bacteria from growing.

enter your bird in competitions, you should exercise it daily. Even if your loft provides an area for flight, your bird still needs to fly freely if it is going to properly develop its homing instinct. Your bird will be fine inside the loft during the day when you are at school, but it will need someone else to care for it if you ever go on vacation.

Keeping the loft clean and dry is the best way to prevent your bird from getting sick. Provide your bird with a small basin for bathing, and change the water often. Other than bath time, your bird should remain bone dry.

Pigeons training for racing need even more exercise than other birds. Racing pigeons must be in proper shape to travel such great distances.

Your bird will help keep its nails in proper shape all on its own. Landing, walking, or perching on rough surfaces (like pavement or cement) grinds nails naturally. If a nail gets too long or starts to curve over the toe, you will need to file it. The safest way to do this is with an emery board.

Never use a rubber band to attach a note or anything else to your bird's leg. Doing so will cut off the blood supply to its foot. This can cause **gangrene** (GANG-green) and make it necessary for a veterinarian to **amputate** (AM-pyoo-tayt) the limb.

An **avian veterinarian** (AY-vee-un veh-truh-NAYR-ee-un) should examine your bird at least once a year. You will also need to take your bird to the vet if it becomes sick. Common signs of illness include sneezing and sitting on the bottom of the cage.

Many racing pigeon owners also use a variety of vitamins and other supplements to keep their birds healthy. Your bird may need some extra vitamins added to its food both before and

funFACTS

Pigeons have great eyesight. Search-and-rescue groups take pigeons in helicopters over the sea. The pigeons can spot orange life jackets before humans can. They are trained to peck a button to alert the rescuers that someone is below.

after a race. Some owners even give their racing pigeons **antibiotics** (an-tih-by-AH-tiks) to prevent illness. Remember, your bird may be very healthy, but it will encounter many other birds when it enters races. Any number of diseases can be passed on to your bird at these times.

It can be very exciting to attend a pigeon race. You may think it would be even more fun to race your own bird. Becoming a racing pigeon owner is a big step, though. Make sure you are ready for it.

BEFORE MAKING UP YOUR MIND

Owning a racing pigeon can be a lot of fun. The competition can be thrilling, and the relationships you make along the way can turn into lifelong friendships. Spending time with others who share your interest also can be a great way to learn even more about this truly unique pet.

Before asking your parents for a racing pigeon, though, you should consider whether this is indeed the right pet for you. Ask yourself the following questions: Do I have the time to properly care for a racing pigeon? Am I willing to put the work into training this pet? Is there a racing pigeon club in my area that I could join? Also, racing pigeons can live a long time. Am I sure I won't become bored with this pet?

If you already own a cat or dog, will you have enough time to care for those pets as well as for your new racing pigeon? In most cases, cats and birds are natural enemies. Even some dogs have a strong bird-hunting instinct. Will it be safe to keep your bird around these other animals?

Even if you answer yes to these questions, your parents may still say no to your request. Although the racing pigeon itself may not be expensive, the loft you must build for your pet will take a lot of time and money. Can you help with the expense? Are you willing to help build this structure?

Your parents also may be concerned that they will get stuck with the responsibilities of feeding your racing pigeon and cleaning up after it. The best way to show your parents that you will in fact be a responsible caregiver is by staying on top of all your current chores. It may be hard to convince your parents that you will keep a pigeon loft clean if your room is usually a mess.

Some people think pigeons shouldn't be raced at all. Certain studies have shown that more than half the birds released do not make it back home. Both you and your parents must decide if the risk of losing your pet is worth taking. If someone finds a lost bird, that person can usually find its owner by checking the animal's band. If a bird is especially shy, though, it may not allow a stranger to get close enough to see this important information.

If you like the look of a racing pigeon, you may enjoy owning a dove instead. You can take your dove outside in a small carrying cage—but it will need a much larger cage inside.

If your parents do say no, the best thing you can do is calmly accept their decision. This will help show them how mature you are. The better you handle their response, the greater the chances will be that they will reconsider your request if you decide to ask again at some point in the future. In the meantime, visit your local racing pigeon club, and learn even more about these exciting birds.

Owning any pet is a big responsibility. Not only do you have to make sure that a racing pigeon is the right pet for you, but you must also be certain that you are right for it. Trust your parents to help you make this awesome decision. They know you better than anyone else in the world.

Books

Blechman, Andrew D. *Pigeons: The Fascinating Saga of the World's Most Revered and Reviled Bird.* New York: Grove Press, 2007.

Clements, John. *Long-Distance Pigeon Racing.* Marlborough, Wiltshire, United Kingdom: Crowood Press, 2007.

Works Consulted

Bissett, Ron. *Pigeon Fancying: Caring, Breeding, Racing, & Exhibiting.* Newton Abbott, Devon, United Kingdom: David & Charles, 1985.

Glover, David. *Racing Pigeons.* Marlborough, Wiltshire, United Kingdom: Crowood Press, 1999.

Nielson, Michael. "Racing Pigeons Bring Friends, Teach Life Lessons." *Cedar City [Utah] Review*, Vol. 2, No. 18, August 24, 2006.

Project Pigeon Watch, Cornell Laboratory of Ornithology—Ithaca, New York; 607-254-2427.

Vriends, Matthew. *Pigeons: Complete Pet Owner's Manual.* New York: Barron's Educational Series, 2005.

Web Addresses

American Dove Association
http://www.doveline.com/

American Racing Pigeon Union
http://www.pigeon.org/

Canadian Racing Pigeon Union
http://www.canadianracingpigeonunion.com/

International Federation: American Homing Pigeon Fanciers, Inc.
http://www.ifpigeon.com/

National Pigeon Association
http://www.npausa.com/

Pigeons in Combat
http://pigeonsincombat.com

Project Pigeon Watch
http://www.birds.cornell.edu/pigeonwatch/

Racing Pigeon Digest
http://www.racingpigeondigest.com/

GLOSSARY

aerodynamic (ayr-oh-dy-NAA-mik)—Having a shape that moves easily through air.

amputate (AM-pyoo-tayt)—To surgically cut off.

antibiotics (an-tih-by-AH-tiks)—Medicine that kills bacteria.

avian veterinarian (AY-vee-un veh-truh-NAYR-ee-un)—Bird doctor.

dehumidifier (dee-hyoo-MIH-duh-fy-er)—A machine that removes moisture from the air.

fancier (FAN-see-er)—A person with an interest in a particular area.

feral (FAYR-ul)—Wild; returned to the wild after having been tamed.

fledge (FLEDJ)—Leave the nest and fly.

gallantry (GAL-un-tree)—Bravery.

gangrene (GANG-green)—The death of body tissue caused by lack of blood to the area.

loft (LAWFT)—An outbuilding that houses cages for animals such as racing pigeons.

morph (MORFS)—The various color and pattern types of pigeons.

reproduction (ree-proh-DUK-shun)—Making babies.

squab (SKWOB)—A young pigeon between 1 and 30 days old.

ventilation (ven-tuh-LAY-shun)—The process of allowing fresh air into an area.

wean (WEEN)—To be able to eat on one's own without the assistance of a parent.

INDEX